What others are saying about Isabelle's Invisible Neighbor

Isabelle's Invisible Neighbor is a story that encourages empathy and social awareness at a time when both are desperately needed in our world. Homelessness is a real issue, yet one that is often brushed aside or not addressed at all with young people. It is so important to provide opportunities for children to consider the needs and feelings of others so they may grow to be kind and able contributors to society. This book provides a gateway for that through its simple story and the discussion questions provided.

Amy Stevenson, Ph.D.
Literacy Specialist

Loving our neighbors—especially those on the margins—is absolutely central to being a follower of Jesus Christ. Unfortunately, there is a dearth of resources to disciple children to care for those whom Jesus loved so deeply: the outcasts, the vulnerable, and the poor. Touching and dignifying, Isabelle's Invisible Neighbor should become a staple in every family's library.

Brian Fikkert
Co-author of *When Helping Hurts: How to Alleviate Poverty without Hurting the Poor...and Yourself*

Hooray for Sandy Furnell for bringing one of society's most exasperating dilemmas down to a child's level. Solving this ever-present problem will take the efforts of everyone, including our youngest generations. They need to be taught the many reasons for homelessness and learn how they can make a difference, one person at a time. This little book is a perfect example of how that can be done.

John Ashmen
President, Citygate Network

ISABELLE'S INVISIBLE NEIGHBOR

WRITTEN BY
Sandy Furnell

ILLUSTRATED BY
Amanda Ravensdale

Isabelle's Invisible Neighbor

Copyright © 2023 by Sandy Furnell
Illustrations by Amanda Ravensdale

Published by Lucid Books in Houston, TX
WWW.LUCIDBOOKS.COM

All rights reserved. No part of this publication may be reproduced, stored in a retrieval system, or transmitted in any form by any means, electronic, mechanical, photocopy, recording, or otherwise, without the prior permission of the publisher, except as provided for by USA copyright law.

Scripture quotations are taken from the Holy Bible, New International Version®, NIV®. Copyright ©1973, 1978, 1984, 2011 by Biblica, Inc.™ Used by permission of Zondervan. All rights reserved worldwide. www.zondervan.com The "NIV" and "New International Version" are trademarks registered in the United States Patent and Trademark Office by Biblica, Inc.™

eISBN: 978-1-63296-581-3
ISBN: 978-1-63296-579-0 (paperback)
ISBN: 978-1-63296-580-6 (hardback)

Special Sales: Most Lucid Books titles are available in special quantity discounts. Custom imprinting or excerpting can also be done to fit special needs. Contact Lucid Books at Info@LucidBooks.com

Like any creative endeavor, this book is the coming together of just the right people and resources at just the right time. As odd as this may sound, I am grateful for the 2020 pandemic. Although it brought much grief and despair, it also brought our busy lives to a halt. In that unexpected pause, we reflected and made space for ideas and emotions to bubble to the surface. Several years ago, I read John Ashmen's *Invisible Neighbors*. It challenged my thinking. During the pandemic, I, like many others, noticed more neighbors, especially the poor and vulnerable. It was during that time that *Isabelle's Invisible Neighbor* was birthed.

I am most grateful to my amazingly creative daughter Olivia, who was the first to read the manuscript. Her insightful editing greatly improved the story by bringing a younger perspective and voice to the dialogue. I dedicate this book to her. Victoria Eich, a beloved friend and accomplished writer, pointed out a couple of holes in the story. I'm thankful for her sharp editor's eyes. Dana Thompson helped me process the nuts and bolts of publishing a book and led me to two experienced children's book editors – Joey Hoelscher and Carol Myers – who sharpened the manuscript's grammar and punctuation and advised on age appropriateness. Amy Stevenson's experience as a longtime elementary school teacher proved invaluable in refining the discussion questions.

None of this work would have been possible, however, without Miracle Hill Ministries. My time working with the ministry and the people I've encountered there through the years have taught me that, truly, "Mercy triumphs over judgment." Special thanks to Jacob Edmisten for giving me the time and space to write; to Ryan Duerk for crafting thought-provoking discussion questions and for reminding me of the dignity of people experiencing homelessness; to Susan Pottberg, Chelsia Allison and Yolanda Campusano-Pilarte for providing helpful feedback; to Minda Shelton whose quiet, gentle spirit and genuine love for women in crisis helped shape this story.
I am forever grateful and changed.

"Today is my favorite day," Isabelle thought. She looked forward to school on Thursdays because each Thursday, Mrs. Johnson gave her fourth grade class a new riddle. Mrs. Johnson sometimes called the riddles brain teasers.

Isabelle wondered why it was ok to tease her brain but not her little brother. But she loved the riddles anyway. And she thought it was especially fun to see who could solve the riddle first, the boys or the girls.

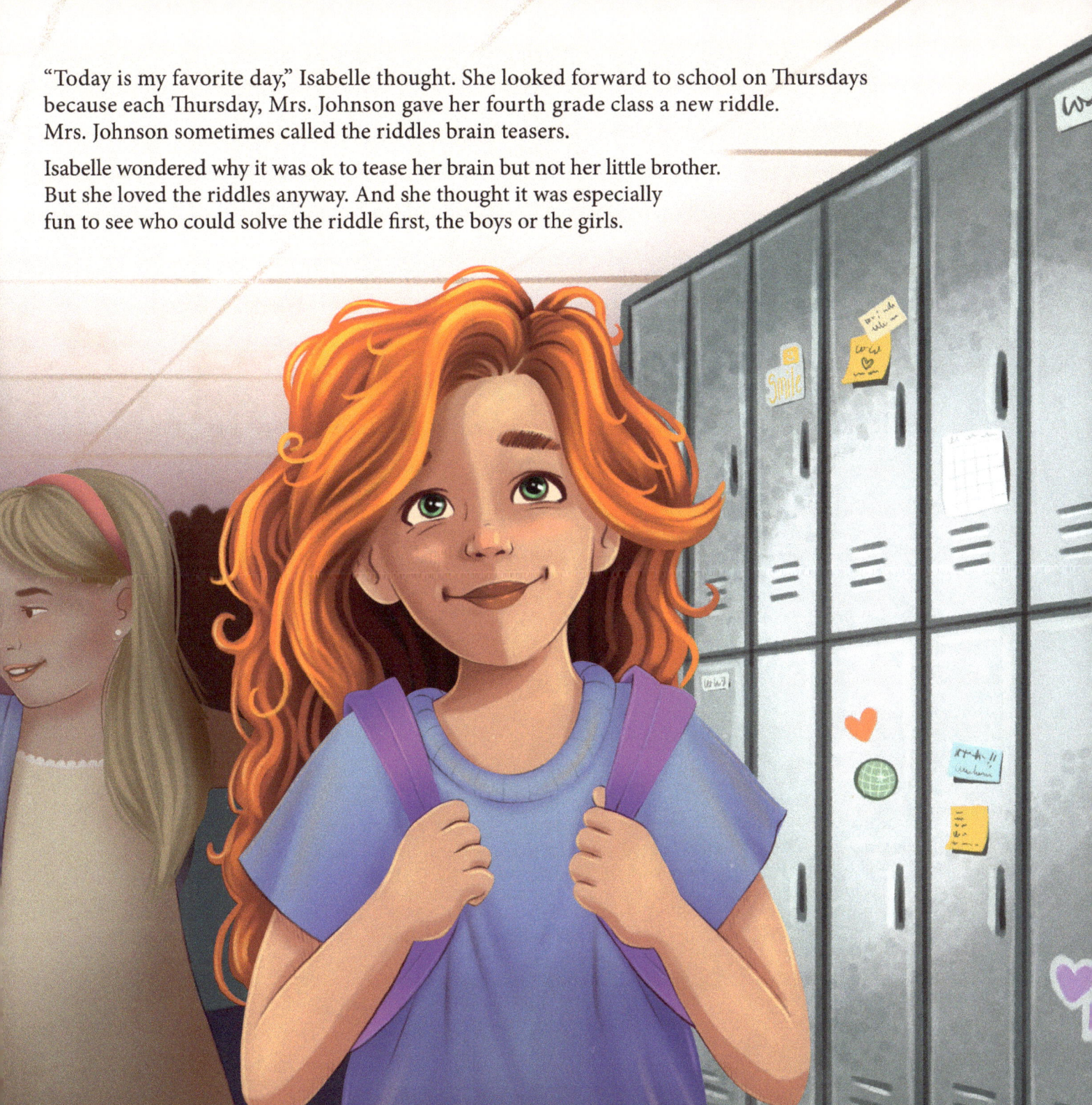

Last Thursday Mrs. Johnson put a piece of paper face down on each student's desk and told the class to flip over their papers at the same time.

They had ten seconds to look at the pictures on the page, then flip it back over and try to remember as much as they could.

"I could only remember six out of the twelve things on my page," Isabelle told her mom that night. "Mostly the animals."

Isabelle hoped to be a veterinarian someday. She had already started practicing her medical skills on the family's Australian Shepherd and enormous Maine Coon cat, Ferdinand. Once she imagined Ferdinand was a puma caught in a hunter's trap, struggling to free his broken leg.

Isabelle knew being a doctor would require quick thinking, so she took Mrs. Johnson's riddles very seriously.

"Today's riddle is going to be a little more challenging," said Mrs. Johnson. "You'll need a few extra days to solve it, and…" Mrs. Johnson paused to make sure everyone was listening attentively. "We're taking a field trip on Monday to give you some clues."

The class cheered and buzzed with excitement. Ethan's hand shot into the air. "Where are we going, Mrs. Johnson?" She replied that it was a surprise and that everyone's parents had already signed the permission slips.

Mrs. Johnson began writing slowly on the board. Isabelle held her breath in anticipation as her teacher carefully formed the first few words of the mysterious riddle. Before Mrs. Johnson could finish, she was interrupted by a knock on the door.

Mr. Sanchez, the school guidance counselor, had brought a new student to the class. "Students, let's welcome Sofia to your class," encouraged Mr. Sanchez. "She just moved here from out of town."

"Hi, Sofia," said some students timidly. Aiden leaned over to his twin brother, Ian, and whispered, "Oooo…Sofia." Sofia blushed as she slipped into the only empty seat, which, unfortunately, was at the front of the room.

"How lucky!" thought Isabelle. "She joined our class on the best day of the week. Maybe she would give the girls an advantage with the riddle." Isabelle liked Sofia's name, too. It sounded mysterious, like her own. Isabelle loved mysteries.

Mrs. Johnson continued writing on the board.

> I am your invisible neighbor.
> I can be here.
> I can be there.
> I make my home just about anywhere.
> Who am I?

"Mrs. Johnson was right," thought Isabelle.
"We've never been given a riddle like this one."

"Copy this week's riddle into your notebooks," said Mrs. Johnson,
"and when you come back to school tomorrow, I want to hear your answers."

As the dismissal bell rang, Isabelle rushed over to Sofia's desk. "I'm Isabelle, but you can call me Izzy. You have such a pretty name. Where are you from?" she asked.

Sofia smiled. She was clearly relieved someone had spoken to her. "I just moved here from Florida," she replied.

Isabelle didn't know much about Florida, but she had read a book about reptiles and knew there were tons of alligators, snakes, and iguanas in Florida. Her curiosity grew as she wondered if Sofia had ever seen one up close.

"Are you busy after school tomorrow?" asked Isabelle. "My mom takes me for ice cream on Fridays and sometimes lets me invite a friend over for the afternoon. Maybe you could come home with me."

Sofia said she would ask her mom and let Isabelle know.

The two girls walked together to the car line where Sofia's mom was waiting for her. As Isabelle waved goodbye to her new friend, she thought about what a wonderful day it had been. She could hardly wait to tell her mom and dad all about Sofia and the mysterious riddle.

Friday couldn't come soon enough for Isabelle. As her classmates trickled in and took their seats, Isabelle eagerly searched for Sofia. Finally, just before the late bell rang, Sofia arrived. She slid a note on Isabelle's desk as she passed by. It read, "My mom said yes." Isabelle beamed with delight at the good news.

After taking attendance, Mrs. Johnson asked if anyone had come up with an answer to the riddle. Michael raised his hand first. "I think invisible neighbors are superheroes," he said. "Like Spiderman or Captain America."

"Or Wonder Woman!" shouted Hannah.

Michael climbed onto his chair, struck a dramatic pose and exclaimed, "Everybody has a favorite superhero. You can't always see them, but you know they're there…kind of like the force with the Jedi."

The class roared with laughter and applauded Michael's idea. Everyone thought his answer was actually pretty good.

Mrs. Johnson said, "Clever thinking, Michael! But no, I'm afraid that's not the answer. Does anyone else have an idea?"

Madison raised her hand next. "There's a creepy, old house in my neighborhood," she said. "Sometimes I see a car parked in front of it, but I never see anyone going in or coming out of the house. I think those are invisible neighbors."

Mrs. Johnson complimented Madison on her creative thinking, but said it wasn't the answer to the riddle. Isabelle, however, wasn't thinking about invisible neighbors at all. She was thinking about ice cream, iguanas, and fun with her new best friend.

That afternoon was even better than Isabelle could have imagined:

bubble gum ice cream
with purple Pop Rocks
that fizzed in her and Sofia's mouths,

jumping on the trampoline
till their legs gave out,

spraying each other and the family dog with the hose,

and, best of all,
Sofia's wild story about being chased
by the iguana that lived in her backyard.

Isabelle knew it would be two whole days before she could see her new friend again and before they would get more clues to the riddle. Her excitement made it nearly impossible to concentrate during church on Sunday.

After a few minutes, however, something the pastor said caught her attention. "Who is my neighbor?" he asked. Isabelle shot straight up in her seat as she recalled Mrs. Johnson's riddle.

The pastor told a story about a man who was beaten up, robbed, and left by the side of the road. Two men passed him by as if he were invisible. When a third man saw him, he stopped and offered to help.

The pastor then asked, "Which of the three was his neighbor?" Isabelle wondered, "How could the first two men see him and not help him?"

When Isabelle arrived at school the next morning, Mrs. Johnson was standing nearby, waiting for her students to check in for the field trip. Isabelle raced over to the yellow school bus so she could save a seat for Sofia.

Once everyone was seated, Mrs. Johnson said, "Remember, I want everyone to be on your best behavior and pay careful attention so you don't miss any of the clues."

The bus rumbled down the road until it finally pulled up in front of a three-story, white brick building. The name on the front said Shepherd's Gate. Isabelle didn't know much about shepherds, but she sure did know a lot about sheep, having read so much about them.

As Isabelle and her classmates walked through the glass doors, they were greeted by a shy boxer with a dark brown coat, stubby tail, and bright pink and green collar.

Soon a woman with a kind face and gentle smile came up behind the dog and introduced herself as the director of Shepherd's Gate.

"Olive loves kids," remarked Ms. Minda. At that moment, Olive let out a strange noise that sounded like a low rumble. Sofia took a step back. "Oh, don't be afraid," Ms. Minda said. "That's how she lets you know she's glad to see you."

The class followed Ms. Minda down a flight of stairs and into a small, simple dining room with a kitchen on one side, much like the one in their school cafeteria. A few women were busily working in the kitchen.

"Raise your hand if you've ever met someone who has experienced homelessness," said Ms. Minda.

Emily raised her hand and said, "My dad and I were in the car one day when we passed by a man holding a sign that said 'Homeless and Hungry. God bless.' But we didn't talk to him and we didn't stop."

After a few minutes, Ms. Minda walked over to the kitchen and came back with a woman who looked a lot like Isabelle's mom. "I want you to meet my friend, Ms. Jenaye," said Ms. Minda. "She works here and is going to tell you more about what it's like to live at Shepherd's Gate."

"Live here?" Isabelle was shocked. "Who lives here?" Ms. Jenaye told the class that Shepherd's Gate is a place where women and children experiencing homelessness can live and get help. She told them that she and her daughter had become homeless after her husband died and she lost her job. Before coming to Shepherd's Gate, they had to live in their car. And when they could afford it, sometimes they stayed in a motel.

"It's really hard to be homeless. It makes you feel like you're alone," said Ms. Jenaye. "We were always tired, hungry, and scared. Sometimes it just felt like we were invisible."

Isabelle's mind raced. Ms. Jenaye went on to say that she and her daughter live in their own house now but she decided to work at Shepherd's Gate so she could help other women like her.

After Ms. Jenaye finished speaking, Ms. Minda said that sometimes we can see people who are homeless, but most of the time we don't. "There are people all around us going through hard times, so how we treat them really matters," she said.

On the way back to school that afternoon, Isabelle and Sofia sat in silence. "What if my mom and I had to live in our car?" Isabelle wondered. She thought about how much she would miss her mom's home-cooked meals, her warm bed, and her pets. Sofia leaned closer and whispered, "Can I tell you a secret?" Isabelle nodded.

"My mom and I live in our car and sometimes we stay with a friend who helps us." she said.

Isabelle was speechless. "How could this be true?" she thought. Before she could respond, Sofia said, "My mom talked to Mr. Sanchez while I was at your house on Friday, and he told her about some homeless shelters we could go to for help. When she told me about it that night, I was scared. But now I think it might be ok for us to go."

Isabelle gave Sofia a long hug. "Can you still come to my house even if you live in a shelter?" Isabelle asked. Sofia smiled and said she hoped she could.

Back in the classroom, Mrs. Johnson asked, "So who is your invisible neighbor?" Before anyone could respond, the dismissal bell rang. It was time to go home.

Home. That word had a whole new meaning for Isabelle.

Isabelle decided to wait for everyone to leave the classroom because she wanted to talk to Mrs. Johnson alone.

"Mrs. Johnson," she said apprehensively. "Sofia told me today that she and her mom live in their car, kind of like the lady at Shepherd's Gate." Mrs. Johnson looked surprised and said, "Thank you for telling me, Isabelle. I'll need to talk with Mr. Sanchez." Isabelle was relieved.

She got quiet and thought for a moment about the riddle. Isabelle finally knew who her invisible neighbor was. Then she asked, "How can I help Sofia?"

Mrs. Johnson smiled and replied, "You already have, Isabelle. You already have."

Discussion Questions

1. What does it mean to experience homelessness?

2. What do you think causes someone to experience homelessness?

3. How do you think it might feel to experience homelessness?

4. What are some feelings Sofia may have experienced throughout the story?

5. Have you ever met someone who was homeless?

    What was it like and what did you think about that person?

6. Why does the story call individuals who experience homelessness our invisible neighbors?

7. Where do you see invisible neighbors in your community?

8. What does it mean to love your neighbor?

9. At the end of the story Mrs. Johnson told Isabelle that she had already helped Sofia.

    What had Isabelle done to help Sofia?

10. If you find out someone is experiencing homelessness, how do you think you could help them?

11. Where could someone go to get help if they are experiencing homelessness?

12. What was your favorite part of the story and why?

Sandy Furnell is a journalist and voiceover artist with a passion for stories that inspire hope and good works. She holds a BS in Communications from Florida International University and has 30+ years' experience in the field. Since 2013, Sandy has been serving in development and communications at Miracle Hill Ministries, a non-profit dedicated to life transformation for people experiencing homelessness. She's learned that poverty can only be overcome by seeing the value and dignity of all people. Sandy and her husband John live in beautiful Upstate South Carolina. She enjoys the outdoors, spending time with family, and sharing tea and conversation with friends.

Connect with her at SandyFurnellMedia@gmail.com.

Miracle Hill Ministries exists that homeless children and adults receive food and shelter with compassion, hear the Good News of Jesus Christ, and move toward healthy relationships and stability.

www.miraclehill.org

To find a faith-focused homeless shelter in your area, like the one Ms. Minda runs, see City Gate Network.

www.citygatenetwork.org

CPSIA information can be obtained
at www.ICGtesting.com
Printed in the USA
LVHW070827010323
740656LV00004B/5